I am not afraid of storms, for I am learning how to sail my ship.

LOUISA MAY ALCOTT

North

West   East

South

©Deb Strain

Be joyful in hope, patient in affliction, faithful in prayer.

THE BOOK OF ROMANS

Hope

Faith

God moves in a mysterious way
His wonders to perform;
He plants His footsteps in the sea
And rides upon the storm.

WILLIAM COWPER

4

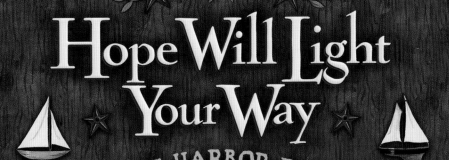

Hope Will Light Your Way

FINDING A SAFE HARBOR FOR YOUR SOUL

PAINTINGS BY **Deb Strain**

HARVEST HOUSE PUBLISHERS

EUGENE, OREGON

Hope Will Light Your Way

Text Copyright © 2003 by Harvest House Publishers
Published by Harvest House Publishers
Eugene, Oregon 97402

ISBN 0-7369-1039-5

Artwork © Deb Strain by arrangement with Mosaic Licensing Inc. It may not be copied or reproduced without permission. For more information regarding artwork featured in this book, please contact:

Mosaic Licensing Inc.
2500 Bisso Lane #200
Concord, CA 94520-4826
(925) 689-9930

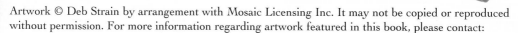

Design and production by Garborg Design Works, Minneapolis, Minnesota

Harvest House Publishers has made every effort to trace the ownership of all poems and quotes. In the event of a question arising from the use of a poem or quote, we regret any error made and will be pleased to make the necessary correction in future editions of this book.

Scripture quotations are taken from the Holy Bible, New International Version®, Copyright © 1973, 1978, 1984 by the International Bible Society. Used by permission of Zondervan Publishing House.

"Hope in the Night" written by Greg Long, Pam Thum, Londa Hentges © 1995 Lehsem Music, LLC, Fresh Rain Music. Used by permission.

Printed in China

03 04 05 06 07 08 09 10 11 / IM / 10 9 8 7 6 5 4 3 2 1

Show me your ways, O LORD, teach me your paths;

guide me in your truth and teach me, for you are God

my savior, and my hope is in you all day long.

One ship sails east and the other west
On the selfsame winds that blow.
'Tis the set of the sails and not the gales
That determine the way they go.

Like the winds of the sea are the ways of fate,
As we voyage along through life;
'Tis the set of the soul that decides the goal
And not the calm or the strife.

ELLA WHEELER WILCOX

God stirs up our comfortable nests, and pushes us over the edge of them, and we are forced to use our wings to save ourselves from fatal falling. Read your trials in this light, and see if your wings are being developed.

HANNAH WHITALL SMITH

Let nothing disturb thee,

Let nothing afright thee.

All things are passing.

God never changes.

ST. THERESA DE AVILA

We must accept finite
disappointment, but we
must never lose infinite hope.

MARTIN LUTHER KING

Hope is a state of mind,
not of the world.
Hope, in this deep and
powerful sense, is not
the same as joy that
things are going well,
or willingness to invest
in enterprises that
are obviously heading
for success, but rather
an ability to work
for something because
it is good.

VACLAV HAVEL

If it were not for hopes, the heart would break.

THOMAS FULLER

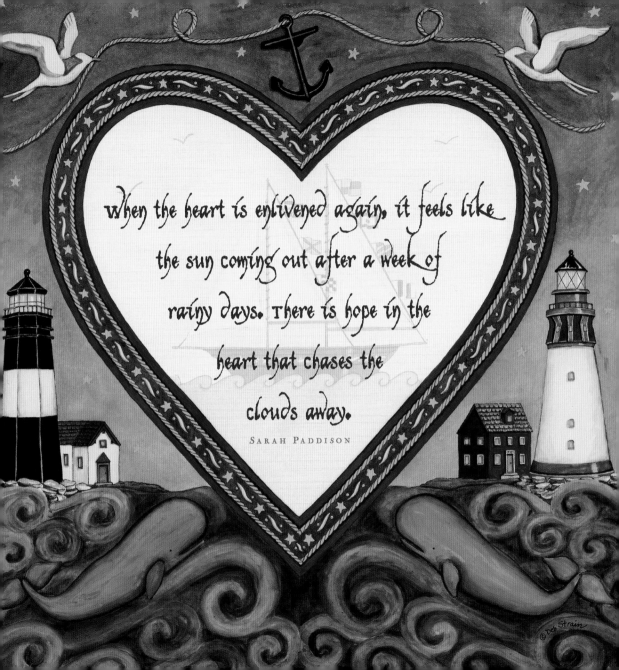

When the heart is enlivened again, it feels like the sun coming out after a week of rainy days. There is hope in the heart that chases the clouds away.

SARAH PADDISON

If you can look at the sunset and smile, then you still have hope. If you can see the good in other people, then you still have hope. If you meet new people with a trace of excitement and optimism, then you still have hope. If you still give people the benefit of the doubt, then you still have hope. If the suffering in others still fills you with pain, then you still have hope. If you still watch love stories or want endings to be happy, then you still have hope. If you can look at the past and smile, then you still have hope. If you still offer your hand of friendship to those who have touched your life, then you still have hope. If you refuse to let a friendship die, or accept that it must end, then you still have very much hope...Hope sees the invisible, feels the intangible, and achieves the impossible.

AUTHOR UNKNOWN

Hope is some extraordinary spiritual grace that God gives us to control our fears, not to oust them.

VINCENT McNABB

I will grant peace in the land, and you will lie down and no one will make you afraid.

THE BOOK OF LEVITICUS

1 1

When the world says, "Give up,"
Hope whispers, "Try it one more time."

ninety~eight percent of what
i worried about never happened.

Hope is faith holding out its hand in the dark.

GEORGE ILES

Life is either a daring adventure or nothing. To keep our faces toward change and behave like free spirits in the presence of fate is strength undefeatable.

HELEN KELLER

SHIP CHANDLER

Hope is putting faith to work when doubting would be easier.

AUTHOR UNKNOWN

Hope is the word which god has written on the brow of every man.

VICTOR HUGO

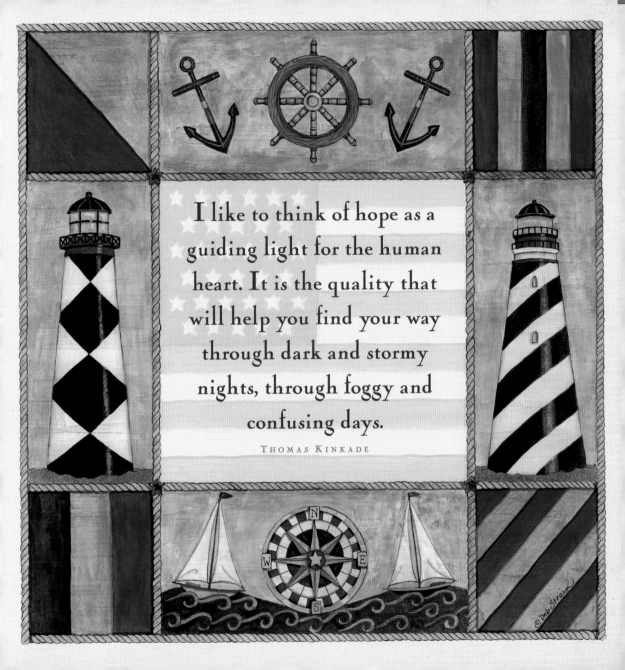

I like to think of hope as a guiding light for the human heart. It is the quality that will help you find your way through dark and stormy nights, through foggy and confusing days.

THOMAS KINKADE

Whatever enlarges hope will also exalt courage.

SAMUEL JOHNSON

Such is hope, heaven's own gift to struggling
mortals, pervading, like some subtle essence
from the skies, all things both good and bad.

CHARLES DICKENS

All which happens in
the whole world happens
through hope. No
husbandman would sow
a grain of corn if he did
not hope it would spring
up and bring forth the
ear. How much more are
we helped on by hope in
the way to eternal life!

MARTIN LUTHER

There is surely a future hope for you,
and your hope will not be cut off.

THE BOOK OF PROVERBS

HOPE LIGHTS THE WAY

Hope, like the glimmering taper's light,

Adorns and cheers the way;

And still as darker grows the night,

Emits a brighter ray.

OLIVER GOLDSMITH

Let this one great, gracious, glorious fact lie in your spirit until it permeates all your thoughts and makes you rejoice even though you are without strength. Rejoice that the Lord Jesus has become your strength and your song — He has become your salvation.

CHARLES SPURGEON

Yet [Abraham] did not waver through unbelief regarding the promise of God, but was strengthened in his faith and gave glory to God, being fully persuaded that God had power to do what he had promised.

THE BOOK OF ROMANS

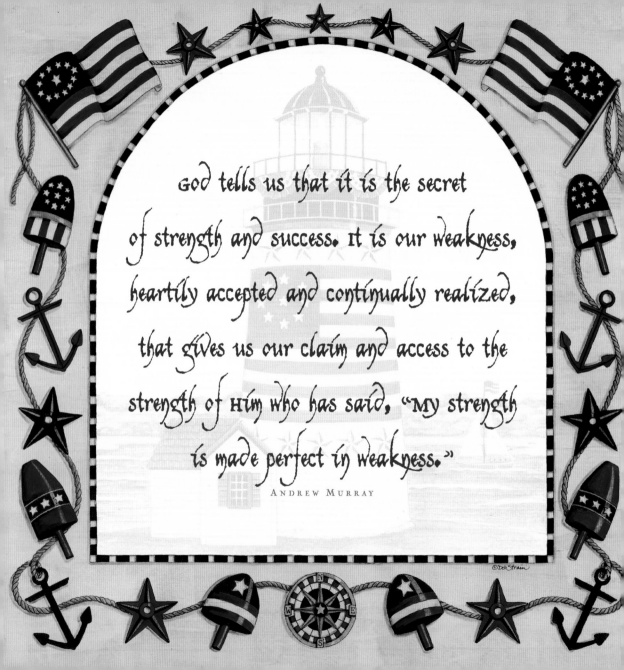

God tells us that it is the secret
of strength and success. It is our weakness,
heartily accepted and continually realized,
that gives us our claim and access to the
strength of Him who has said, "My strength
is made perfect in weakness."

ANDREW MURRAY

Now faith is
being sure of what
we hope for and
certain of what
we do not see.

THE BOOK OF HEBREWS

Quite often we look at a task and think there is no way
we can do what needs to be done. That happens because
we look at ourselves when we should be looking at God.

JOYCE MEYER

what lies behind us and what lies before us are small matters compared to what lies within us.

When the great oak is straining in the wind, the boughs drink in new beauty, and the trunk sends down a deeper root on the windward side. Only the soul that knows the mighty grief can know the mighty rapture. Sorrows come to stretch out spaces in the heart for joy.

EDWIN MARKHAM

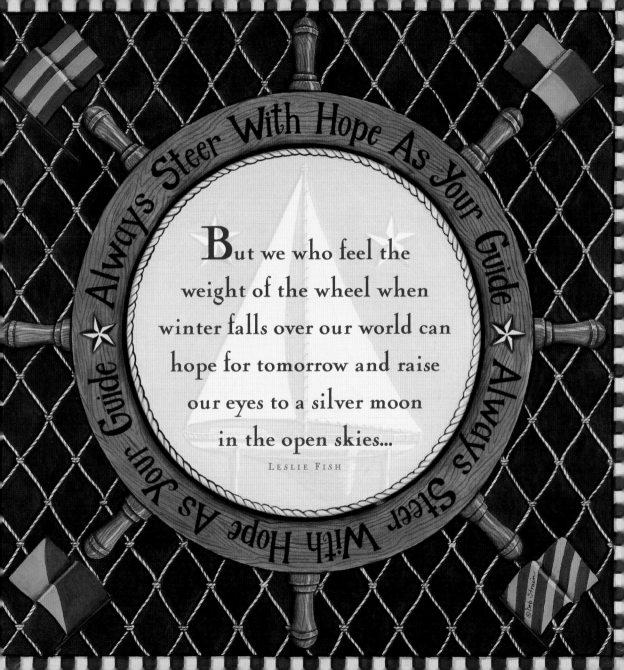

Always Steer With Hope As Your Guide

But we who feel the weight of the wheel when winter falls over our world can hope for tomorrow and raise our eyes to a silver moon in the open skies...

LESLIE FISH

You gain strength, courage, and confidence by each experience in which you really stop to look fear in the face. You are able to say to yourself, "I have lived through this horror. I can take the next thing that comes along."

ELEANOR ROOSEVELT

Hope ever urges on and tells us tomorrow will be better.

TIBULLUS

It is during our darkest

moments that we must

focus to see the light.

AUTHOR UNKNOWN

Nothing is so strong as
gentleness; nothing so
gentle as real strength.

ST. FRANCIS DE SALES

All the strength and force of man comes from his faith in things unseen. He who believes is strong; he who doubts is weak. Strong convictions precede great actions.

JAMES FREEMAN CLARKE

We are made strong by what we overcome.

JOHN BURROUGHS

One who gains strength by overcoming obstacles

possesses the only strength which can overcome adversity.

ALBERT SCHWEITZER

The strength of a man consists in finding out the way God is going, and going that way.

HENRY WARD BEECHER

I believe in prayer. It's the best way we have to draw strength from heaven.

JOSEPHINE BAKER

Do not anticipate trouble, or worry about
what may never happen. Keep in the sunlight.

BENJAMIN FRANKLIN

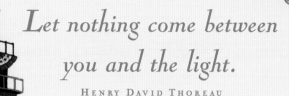

Let nothing come between you and the light.

HENRY DAVID THOREAU

Joy is a light that fills you with hope and faith and love.

ADELA ROGERS ST. JOHNS

Never fear shadows. They simply mean there's a light shining somewhere nearby.

RUTH E. RENKEL

The flowers take the tears
of the weeping night
And give them to the sun
for the day's delight.

JOSEPH SEAMON COTTER, JR.

There are two ways of spreading light:
To be the candle or the mirror that reflects it.

EDITH WHARTON

We wait in hope for the LORD; he is our help and our shield. In him our hearts rejoice, for we trust in his holy name. May your unfailing love rest upon us, O LORD, even as we put our hope in you.

THE BOOK OF PSALMS

To finish the moment, to find the journey's end in every step of the road, to live the greatest number of good hours, is wisdom.

RALPH WALDO EMERSON

HOPE LIGHTS THE WAY

There is hope in the night when the darkness hides the day;

Hope for your heart when the fears hide your faith.

Listen to the one who says everything will be all right.

Don't give up! There is hope in the night.

GREG LONG
"HOPE IN THE NIGHT"

Hope is not prognostication. It is an orientation of the spirit, an orientation of the heart; it transcends the world that is immediately experienced, and is anchored somewhere beyond its horizons.

VACLAV HAVEL

Peace is a journey of a thousand miles and it must be taken one step at a time.

LYNDON B. JOHNSON

Eternity is the divine treasure house, and hope is the window, by means of which mortals are permitted to see, as through glass darkly, the things which God is preparing.

WILLIAM MOUNTFORD

Prayer increases our ability to accept the present moment. You cannot live in the future, you cannot live in the past, you can only live in the now. The present moment is already exactly as it ought to be, even if we do not understand why it is as it is.

MATTHEW KELLY

HoW can god direct our steps if we're not taking any?

SARAH LEAH GRAFSTEIN

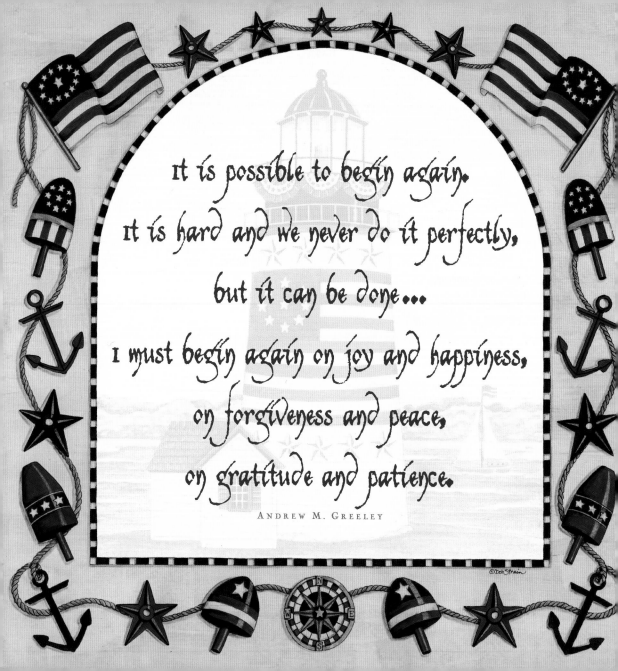

It is possible to begin again.

It is hard and we never do it perfectly,

but it can be done...

I must begin again on joy and happiness,

on forgiveness and peace,

on gratitude and patience.

ANDREW M. GREELEY

Love is the beacon
that guides us through
life's storms.

Hope and patience are two sovereign remedies for all, the
surest reposals, the softest cushions to lean on in adversity.

ROBERT BURTON

Do not look forward to the changes and chances of this life in fear; rather look to them with full hope that, as they arise, God, whose you are, will deliver you out of them. He has kept you hitherto — do you but hold fast to His dear hand, and He will lead you safely through all things; and, when you cannot stand, He will bear you in his arms. Do not look forward to what may happen tomorrow; the same everlasting Father who cares for you today will take care of you tomorrow, and every day. Either He will shield you from suffering, or He will give you unfailing strength to bear it. Be at peace, then, and put aside all anxious thoughts and imaginations.

ST. FRANCIS DE SALES

Steadfast, serene, immovable, the same,
Year after year, through all the silent night
Burns on forevermore that quenchless flame,
Shine on that inextinguishable light!

HENRY WADSWORTH LONGFELLOW
"THE LIGHTHOUSE"

Life is a voyage and home, its safe harbor.

North
West   East
South

As I cross on life's tumultuous seas,
Sailing from earth to Heaven's bright shore,
Christ is like a mighty lighthouse,
Helping me to navigate my course.

He guides me safely through tides of temptation,
Over dangerous reefs of sin,
Lighting my way through dark troubled waters,
'Til the glorious port of Heaven I win.

AUTHOR UNKNOWN

The great revolving light on the cliff at the channel
flashed warm and golden against the clear northern sky,
a trembling, quivering star of good hope.

L.M. MONTGOMERY
ANNE'S HOUSE OF DREAMS

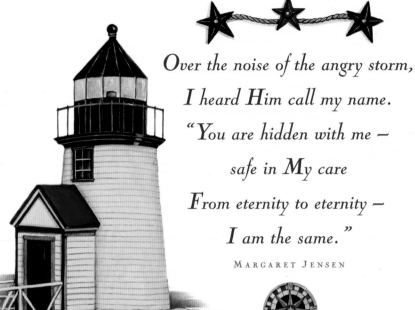

Over the noise of the angry storm,
I heard Him call my name.
"You are hidden with me —
safe in My care
From eternity to eternity —
I am the same."

MARGARET JENSEN

...God, as promised, proves to
be mercy clothed in light.

JANE KENYON

The scene was more beautiful far to the eye,
than if the day in its pride had arrayed it.
And o'er them the lighthouse looked lovely
as hope—the star of life's tremulous ocean.

PAUL MOON JAMES

HOPE LIGHTS THE WAY

He who appoints the sun
to shine by day, who decrees the moon
and stars to shine by night, who stirs up the sea so
that its waves roar — the Lord Almighty is his name.

THE BOOK OF JEREMIAH

His light, through me,
will glow as a beacon for others.

JOHN C. THIBOS

O may the Holy Spirit enable us to keep the beacon-fire blazing, to warn you of the rocks, shoals, and quicksands which surround you, and may He ever guide you to Jesus.

CHARLES SPURGEON

We must build our faith not on fading lights
but on the Light that never fails.

OSWALD CHAMBERS

There is only one light that never goes out.
It comes from God. His light is the true light.
STORMIE OMARTIAN

*Be strong and take
heart, all you who
hope in the LORD.*
THE BOOK OF PSALMS

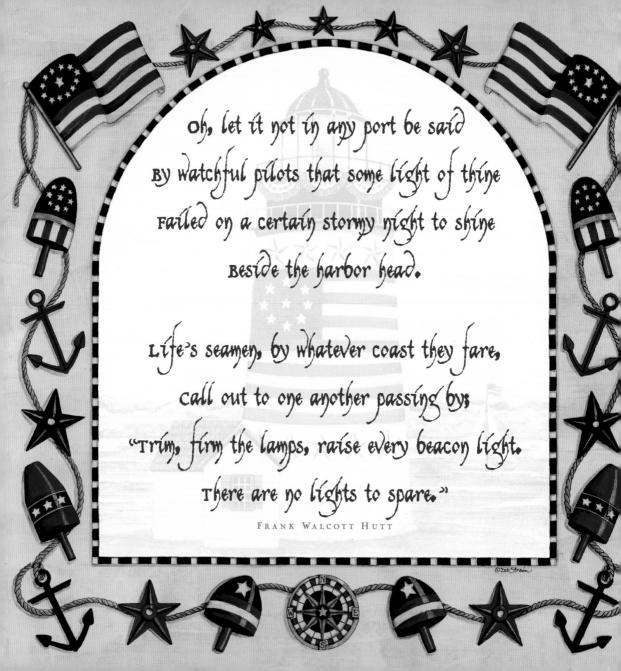

Oh, let it not in any port be said
By watchful pilots that some light of thine
Failed on a certain stormy night to shine
Beside the harbor head.

Life's seamen, by whatever coast they fare,
Call out to one another passing by;
"Trim, firm the lamps, raise every beacon light.
There are no lights to spare."

FRANK WALCOTT HUTT